COUPONING FOR THE BEGINNER :

A Guide to Couponing for the Uninitiated

By Jenny Dean

Disclaimer

The information contained in this guide is for informational purposes only.

I am a couponer. Any advice that I give is my opinion based on my own experiences. You should always read coupon policies and ask store managers of a specific store about using coupons if there is any doubt in your mind about a transaction.

Please understand that there are some links contained in this guide that if you click on them, I may benefit from financially (because they are affiliate links).

The material in this guide may include information, products or services by third parties. Third Party Materials comprise of the products and opinions expressed by their owners. As such, I do not assume responsibility or liability for any Third Party material or opinions.

The publication of such Third Party Materials does not constitute my guarantee of any information, instruction, opinion, products or services contained within the Third Party Material. The use of recommended Third Party Materials does not guarantee any success and/or earnings related to you. Publication of such Third Party Material is simply a recommendation and an expression of my own opinion of that material.

No part of this publication shall be reproduced, transmitted, or sold in whole or in part in any form, without the prior written consent of the author. All trademarks and registered trademarks appearing in this guide are the property of their respective owners.

Users of this guide are advised to do their own due diligence when it comes to making decisions about couponing and all information, products, services that have been provided should be independently verified by you. By reading this guide, you agree that I and my website, GuideToCouponing.com, are not responsible for the success or failure of your couponing decisions relating to any information presented in this Couponing for the Beginner: A Guide to Couponing for the Uninitiated.

Table of Contents

Couponing for the Beginner: A Guide to Couponing for the Uninitiated is the first in a series of books that I will be releasing on GuideToCouponing.com. For over 10 years, I have not only studied, but read, heard and experienced how to coupon legally and effectively.

Much of what I experienced couponing is what I will talk about in this book – I will teach you coupon basics and how everything works. In many ways it was difficult to keep this book relatively short. However, I wanted to stick to the main How To understanding rather than getting into some of the particulars – in those sections where I didn't think it was necessary to expand, I went ahead and linked to an article on the Internet where you can learn more about a particular subject.

Please enjoy this book and let me know if there are things you disagree with or if there are subjects you think I could expand on or make improvements on.

I do ask that you please keep this book to yourself. I have spent years not only researching and gathering information but actually writing the book as well. My interest in selling this book is so that I can dedicate more of my time researching better deals and ways to save you more money as well.

Note for Hard Copy Readers: If you contact me at info@guidetocouponing.com I will send you a digital version of the book (in PDF form) that has all the clickable links - so that you don't have to spend your time searching and typing in links, rather you can just click through!

If you haven't already, I encourage you to subscribe to GuideToCouponing.com's newsletter.

I n recent years, due to our economic recession, couponing has enjoyed a resurgence. While the economy may be improving, many Americans are still couponing because they realize that they can save thousands of dollars a year by couponing and even make money from couponing. In fact, there are ways to get your favorite products for pennies or even for free. This *Couponing for the Beginner: A Guide to Couponing for the Uninitiated* will help you understand how it all works, why it works and prepare you for your life as a couponer.

I personally love coupons; otherwise I wouldn't be writing and publishing this book! My mom couponed when I was a little girl – on Sunday mornings, I loved sitting at the kitchen table cutting coupons out for my mom for the week. When I quit my corporate job five years ago and started by own business, I had to figure out how to budget better since my income was so irregular. While I had used coupons sporadically for years, it wasn't until my income became unpredictable that I really looked into how to effectively coupon. I started researching couponing on the Internet and quickly discovered how much money you can save and MAKE by using coupons effectively.

I think of coupons as cash. There's really no other way to think of them. In fact, at my local grocery store, I have made a purchase, forgotten to use a coupon and gone to customer service to re-do the transaction only to find that they just give me cash for the coupon! In other words, if the coupon was for $1 off of a product, they just open the register and hand me a dollar rather than redoing the transaction. That was the first time that I really saw the value of a coupon as pure CASH! I don't suggest this as a strategy, but wanted to give you an idea of a coupon's value. *Every time I save a dollar on a tube of toothpaste, it's a dollar that I didn't have to spend!*

Whether you want to learn how to coupon to save money on your favorite brands or if you are looking to become a crazy couponer, *Couponing for the Beginner: A Guide to Couponing for the Uninitiated* will show you the way.

The purpose of *Couponing For The Beginner: A Guide To Couponing For The Uninitiated* is to teach you HOW TO use coupons to boost your bottom line. You'll learn what coupons are, how to use them effectively, how to bring home your first real deal and about websites that do coupon matchups for specific deals and more.

Chapter 1

What Are Coupons? – Manufacturer and Store Coupons

More than likely you already know what coupons are, otherwise, I doubt you would have purchased this book. Nonetheless, in an effort to be as thorough as possible, I wanted to cover what coupons are and perhaps you will learn something new anyway!

Here's what Wikipedia has to say, "A coupon is a ticket or document that can be exchanged for a financial discount or rebate when purchasing a product." Then they go on to say, "Customarily, coupons are issued by manufacturers of consumer

packaged goods or by retailers, to be used in retail stores as a part of sales promotions. They are often widely distributed through mail, coupon envelopes, magazines, newspapers, the Internet, directly from the retailer, and mobile devices such as cell phones. Since only price-conscious consumers are likely to spend the time to claim the savings, coupons function as a form of price discrimination, enabling retailers to offer a lower price only to those consumers who would otherwise go elsewhere. In addition, coupons can also be targeted selectively to regional markets in which price competition is great."

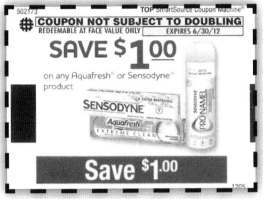

Coupons can be created by manufacturers, store chains, local businesses and more. I have included images of coupons in this chapter – the first one is a store coupon for Target that gives you $5 off when you purchase 2 Purina brand pet care items. The other one is a manufacturer's coupon, issued by the manufacturer to save $1 off of Sensodyne or Aquafresh toothpastes. This coupon is actually called a Blinkie (as it was pulled from a Blinkie machine in an aisle at a store) – you will learn more about those in Chapter 2.

- -

Coupon Language

As with any hobby, couponing has its own language. Here's a quick rundown of common terms used among couponers and ones that you will see on the match-up sites where they work out deal scenarios for you. So feel free to use this as a reference guide.

- BOGO = Buy One Get One
- B1G1 = Buy One Get One
- B2G1 = Buy Two Get One Free
- BLINKIE: a coupon you get from a Blinkie machine – which are little (usually) red coupon dispenser machines that are located in grocery aisles – older ones have blinking red lights, but newer ones sometimes don't.
- CATALINA: manufacturer coupons that print out from a little machine at the register, triggered by what you buy. They come out in long strips similar to a cash tape. The checker should hand them to you with your receipt. They used to be red and white, but some are now printing in color. Some catalinas are very valuable because they give the equivalent of cash on your next purchase. For example, you might receive a $1 catalina for buying 2 P&G products. The $1 catalina will be good on anything the next time you shop. Catalinas are a big deal; Walgreens has lots of specials offering catalinas (which they call 'Register Rewards')
- CPN = Coupon
- ECB = ExtraCare Bucks from CVS

- GC = Giftcard
- MBG = Money Back Guarantee
- MIR = Mail-in Rebate
- MM = Money Maker
- OOP = Out of Pocket
- RP = RedPlum Coupon Inserts
- SAE = Self Addressed Envelope
- SASE = Self Addressed Stamped Envelope
- SMP = Specialty Marked Packages
- SS = SmartSource Coupon Inserts
- TMF = Try Me Free
- WYB = When You Buy
- EXP = Expiration date of coupon
- X = Expiration date of coupon, sometimes written like x6/28 – meaning that the coupon expires on 6/28

Chapter 3

Coupon Rules And Policies

One of the most important things to do when couponing is to follow the rules. There are "rules" listed on every coupon and people that abuse those rules, have suffered the consequences – some have even spent time in jail. As long as you follow the rules, then you will stay out of trouble and more importantly, help keep manufacturers producing coupons. In other words, as long as the system isn't abused, then it should continue to be offered. You are an important step in keeping the system alive, so be sure to be conscious of the rules.

Here are some of the general rules:

1. **One coupon per item purchased –** in other words, you cannot use two 35 cent Colgate coupons on one tube of Colgate. There are exceptions to this rule however. For example, you might have a manufacturer's coupon that gives you $3 off WYB 2 products. In that case, you could only use one manufacturer coupon for those two items purchased.

   GuidetoCouponing.com Reader Emily says, "Bed Bath and Beyond allows you to use expired coupons and will tell you the best deal for you _ how many $% coupons and how many 20% off."

2. **Expiration dates –** be sure to check expiration dates and do not use expired coupons unless, of course, the store where you're using them accepts them.

3. **Size Requirements –** because of shows like TLC's Extreme Couponing, manufacturers are buckling down on size requirements. If a coupon is for a 20 oz. bottle of Dawn or larger – be sure to get the 20 oz or larger size.

Other common rules include:

- Limit one coupon per purchase or item (be careful on these – there's a difference between one coupon per item and one coupon per transaction, when in doubt ask the store manager. Cashiers don't always know and sometimes like to invent their own rules. You can also always call the corporate offices of the store where you are wanting to use the coupon, as they always know.)
- Void if sold, exchanged or transferred
- Coupon value may not exceed value of item purchased
- No cash value

Coupon Policies

It's important to understand a store's coupon policy. Below is a list of coupon policies for popular coupon match up stores:

- CVS Coupon Policy
- Target's Coupon Policy
- Wal-mart Coupon Policy
- Rite-Aid Coupon Policy
- Walgreens Coupon Policy

I frequently coupon at CVS, so I print out their coupon policy and keep it with me in my accordion file (discussed in Chapter 7). It's important to have a coupon policy on hand for any cashiers who decide they want to make up the store's coupon policy.

Chapter 4

Why Coupons Exist

You might be wondering why manufacturers and stores go to the effort to even have coupons – considering all the steps involved (and these probably don't cover all the steps involved):

- Figuring out the discount to offer and on which of their products
- Having a graphic designer design the coupon ad
- Having a copywriter write the copy for the coupon ad
- Paying a company like RedPlum or SmartSource to put it in their inserts
- Paying stores like CVS to send in the coupons redeemed to a coupon clearing house for processing
- Paying the people at coupon clearing house for processing
- ...and so on and so forth

And yet, they continue to issue coupons. So there has to be a benefit to them, right? Right.

Here are some of the reasons why manufacturers and stores issue coupons:

- To increase brand awareness
- To increase sales of certain products
- To encourage consumers to try products
- To encourage consumers to change brands

Stores accept coupons because they not only receive the face value of the coupon, but they are also reimbursed a handling fee for accepting the coupon in the first place. Such a fee (usually between 8¢-12¢/coupon) covers the cost of redemption of the coupon. So if you think of a huge corporate chain like CVS, for example, who might submit a million coupons a month to coupon clearing houses – they'll earn a profit of over $80,000-$120,000 for the month. Seems like it's worth it to me!

Of course, another reason for a store like CVS to accept coupons is to attract people like us who want to shop at places that accept coupons!

If you want to read more about this topic, Erica at iheartcvs.com does a great job explaining everything.

Chapter 5

Where To Get Coupons

There are a number of places to acquire coupons and where you search might depend on what sort of coupons you need or want. For example, if you are looking for those shiny Sunday inserts, you can get a bunch of your local papers from a newsstand, you can ask your family, friends and neighbors to save them for you, you can collect them from recycle bins (either from the end of everyone's driveways or from those huge paper recycling bins usually by schools), buy them from an online clipping source, buy them from a person you find online or buy them on eBay.

Because of TV shows like Extreme Couponing and the higher number of people couponing in recent years, some stores are limiting the number of newspapers you can buy in one visit.

Below is a list of the different kinds of coupons and where you can source them:

Sunday Newspaper Coupon Inserts - Red Plum, SmartSource, General Mills and Proctor and Gamble inserts.

- Your local Sunday paper
- Recycle bins in your neighborhood
- Paper Recycle Dumpster Bins
- Ask friends, family and neighbors to save them for you

- Online Clipping Services like CouponDede.com
- eBay
- Online trading boards like RMCSellers or rmctraders Yahoo! Groups

Parade Magazine – this usually appears in the Sunday paper and along with various articles, it can be sprinkled with coupons.

Printable Online Coupons

- Coupons.com
- Red Plum
- SmartSource
- Individual Manufacturer's websites
- Store Websites
- Home Made Simple
- Coolsavings.com
- Albertsons.com
- Couponsurfer.com

- Eversave.com – Eversave.com a great deal site with one local deal a day up to 90 Percent off. And if you join now you'll get $10 off any deal.
- Kroger.com
- BoxTops4Education.com
- BettyCrocker.com
- Eclip.com
- Pillsbury.com
- EatBetterAmerica.com
- ValPak.com
- Target.com
- CVS.com
- Couponnetwork.com
- CellFire.com – this site offers both printable coupons and digital ones.

Magazines – a lot of monthly magazines have coupons when a manufacturer has advertised in the publication. They will include a coupon in the ad as an additional incentive for you to try/buy their product.

- **All You** – a monthly magazine that has more or less $100 worth of coupons per magazine. I like the 2-year subscription because it's cheaper overall.
- Baby Magazines
- People

Digital Coupons

- CellFire.com – This site offers both printable coupons and digital ones. Once you enter your store loyalty card number, you can then select coupons to add to that card and when your card is scanned at the store, those coupons will be subtracted from the total (assuming you bought the products needed to use the coupons). They have deals for non-grocery stores too like Sears.
- SavingStar - SavingStar is a fully digital, grocery eCoupon service – it's based online and also available on iPhone and Android mobile apps. There's nothing to clip, nothing to print. Every week/month, SavingStar offers eCoupons redeemable at over 24,000 grocery and drug stores throughout the country, SavingStar's eCoupons are linked to your customer loyalty card at different stores (for example, mine is linked with my CVS card and my local grocery store card). SavingStar's eCoupons are a different kind of coupon – because you can use a manufacturer's coupon, a store coupon and a SavingStar eCoupon all on the same purchase. After you load their coupons on your reward card and then go buy that specific item at

the store, SavingStar automatically adds the value of each eCoupon redeemed into users' SavingStar accounts, enabling them to pick their payout from cash to gift cards to charity donations.

Mailers

- P&G Everyday Savings Booklet
- Home Made Simple – this is a P&G website
- RedPlum

Specially Marked Packages – manufacturers sometimes stuff coupons into boxes of their other products (much like the photo of the Tampax Radiant box below, offering $5 in coupons on the inside). They usually announce it on the front of the package where the coupons are located. Sometimes there are coupons inside without there being any notification of it – so be sure to check the box and literature of anything you buy before throwing it away.

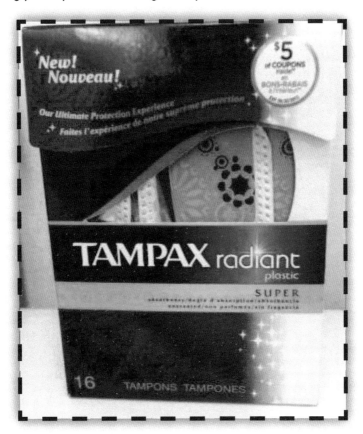

Newspapers – in addition to the Sunday newspaper inserts, you can find many coupons for local businesses as well as manufacturers' coupons in your daily newspapers.

Catalinas - many major grocery store chains as well as some of the super store chains have coupons that print out at checkout from a small machine next to the register. They usually are printed in red and black or in full color. They typically print because they are tied to your purchases - for example, if you have purchased a bunch of baby products at Target, then you might receive a coupon for $1 off Pampers wipes on your next visit. In other words, they see that you are shopping for a baby, so they want to bring you back to the store the next time, so they offer you something you might need again. The store (Target) and manufacturer (Pampers) work together for these kinds of promos. Sometimes those coupons can be $3 off your next baby purchase of $10 or more. In other words, sometimes they are not tied to a specific product, but rather they are tied to a specific category of products.

Blinkie Machines - these are red machines that are usually located in the grocery store aisles and sometimes even in major pharmacy store chains and many super store chains. Sometimes when someone has pulled a coupon from a Blinkie machine and they don't want it, then they will put it in a slot at the top of the machine - so be sure to look for discarded ones there. Below is a photo of a Blinkie Machine at a CVS store and there is also an image of a Blinkie coupon to the right.

Peel Off/Instant Coupons – these are the kind that are attached to the bottle or product you are buying – like the 55¢ coupons on the bottles of ACT mouthwash below. All you have to do is peel it off and use it at the register.

Hang Tag Coupons – these usually hang on the bottle of a product. You can see an example of one below on the bottle of Odwalla.

Tear Pads – a pad or stack of coupons stuck to the shelves or located on product special displays or on refrigerator or freezer doors.

Demo People – when a company hires a person to do a promo in a store, often times they have coupons that they can hand out. If they aren't visible – ask them if they have any. Same goes for people that are stocking shelves in stores – if they work for the manufacturer as a rep, then they will probably have coupons with them. Ask and you shall receive!!

Through the Mail – you can always write your favorite brands and ask them if they can send you coupons. This is easily done through an email – be sure to include your name and address.

Members Only - Some manufacturers have member only sections of their websites (like in the SoftScrub.com example below) where they allow you to sign up for an account and people with an account get even better offers for coupons - instead of $1 off a product, for example, you might get a B1G1 coupon as a member.

Facebook Pages - A lot of the stores and the manufacturers like to offer coupons, free samples, try me free on new products that they launch, etc. on their Facebook pages. Be sure to like your favorite brands on Facebook and follow them to find out about any special offers.

Once you are a serious couponer, you'll want to have multiple copies of the Sunday paper inserts so that if there is a sale or a deal on your favorite item, you are stocked up on the coupons and are ready to go when the sale happens. For example, I get 10 copies of every Sunday paper insert; so that I always know I have enough.

Every area of the country is a little bit different as to where the coupons go when the Sunday papers are not sold, so be sure to check with your newspaper carrier to find out where the surplus coupon inserts go. Of course, as I said before, you can always ask family and friends to help you or walk your neighborhood on recycle day. My neighborhood's recycle day happens to be on Monday – so people usually lay their Sunday paper right on the very top, so it's easy to find! Another idea is that if you are looking to coupon for your church, for example, then you could ask the members of your congregation to bring in their Sunday papers for you. Part of couponing is being resourceful and creative to get better deals and steals.

Chapter 6

Where To Buy Coupons - Is It Illegal To Buy Or Sell Coupons?

It is illegal to buy and sell coupons. On most manufacturer's coupons, in the fine print, you will notice that it says something like, "Coupon is void if altered, transferred, exchanged, sold or auctioned, copied or if prohibited by law." Yet, there are many coupon clipping service sites as well as people on eBay that sell them – so why is it allowed?

Well, the coupon clipping service sites get around these laws by saying that the fees for the coupons cover their cost for clipping, grouping, managing and mailing the coupons. Many sellers on eBay write something like, "The coupons are FREE! You are paying us for our coupon clipping service. Fees are for the time it takes for us to locate, sort, cut, and ship these coupons to you!" in the description of their auction to cover their liability.

From GuidetoCouponing.com Reader Lisa, "I am a moderator for a mommy group in my local area and we have a "Coupon Train". One person starts it by putting together all her unwanted clipped coupons and puts it in a mailer with a list of all the mom's addresses that want to participate. She mails it to the next person on the list. The next person gets it and takes the coupons she wants and adds any clipped coupons she won't use to the pile and mails the entire envelope and list to the next person listed below her. Our Coupon Train has been going on for over 5 years and I love it!)"

Popular Coupon Clipping Services:

- CouponDede.com
- The Coupon Master
- The Coupon Clippers

I include more coupon clipping services in the resource section at the end of this book.

Another option is to trade coupons. If there is a group of you that are getting into couponing or if you have a friend or a relative who you want to trade with – you can always do that as well. There are also coupon trading boards through websites like RefundCents.

There are many people out there who are willing to trade coupons for cash or for other coupons. RefundCents.com, for example, has a Yahoo! Group - RMCSellers or rmctraders Yahoo! Groups - where you can post coupons you have for trade as well as coupons you want to trade.

You can read more about buying and selling coupons on About.com.

Chapter 7

How To Organize Your Coupons

Organizing Coupons to Store at Home:

Collecting and organizing coupons is one of the essential steps when learning how to coupon effectively. Part of the coupon game is learning how to effectively organize your coupons so that you are not spending hours and hours sorting through all of them in the store or at home.

I cannot stress enough the importance of organization. With the advent of the Internet, it is now easier than ever to find coupons for products on sale, especially if the coupons are in their original inserts or even if they are organized in a coupon binder.

I recommend the following set up (as seen in the YouTube video here) to keep your Sunday inserts organized.

Here are links to the file box and the folders featured in the YouTube video above:

- United Solutions Snap and Lock Plastic File Tote
- Smead Hanging File Folders, Letter Size, 1/5 Cut Tab, Assorted Colors, 25 Per Box

Organizing Coupons for the Store:

When going to the store, I do not lug around my plastic file box. Rather I use an extended file organizer (an accordion file) that I got on clearance at CVS – it has convenient dividers already built in. You can buy it on Amazon.com for less than $10.

You might have seen folks on the Extreme Couponing show use 3-ring binders as well. They use 3-ring binders with baseball card storage like insert pages to help stuff the coupons inside.

A quick search on Amazon.com helped me find those pages – here they are 20 (Twenty Pages) - Pro 3-Pocket Coupon Storage Pages (3 Horizontal 3 1/2 x 8 inch Sized Top Loaded Slots). Looks like they have a bunch of different styles of pages for your convenience.

Categories for Organizing Your Coupons

Another way to organize your coupons is by categories. Here's a list of categories you could consider using for your coupon binder or accordion file. Of course, if one of the categories listed below does not apply to your household – for instance, if your kids are past the baby stage, then you don't have to keep a category for baby products.

Baby Products	Dairy/Cheese	Medicines
Baking (cakes, muffins, etc.)	Dental (Toothpaste/Brush/Mouthwash)	Oil/Shortening
Beverages	Deodorant	Paper Products
Body (lotions, make up)	Dessert	Pasta
Bread	Frozen Foods	Pets
Candy	Hair	Plastic Bags
Canned/Jar Products	Household (film, batteries, light bulbs)	Seasoning
Cat Food	Instant Dinners	Soaps
Cereal	Laundry/Detergent	Soup
Cleaning	Meat	Tampons/Pads
Cookies	Rice	
Crackers	Snacks	

Most people cut every coupon in categories of products that they use and forget brand loyalty. Of course, if you are just looking to save on your favorite brands and not looking to get them for free – then stick with your brand loyalty.

But the idea is, if you use canned tomatoes, then cut ALL canned tomato coupons including all brands Del Monte, Best Choice, etc., you get my drift.

I like to clean out my expired coupons once a month - some coupons expire within weeks of being issued, whereas others expire within months of being issued. Recycle all expired coupons in your paper recycle bin, so that they can be made to make more coupons!

IMPORTANT! Be sure to put your name, address, telephone number and email address (or any of those things listed that you feel comfortable with) on your coupon binder or accordion file - that way if you lose it, there's a chance you just might have it returned to you.

Mine says:

If lost, please contact:

Jenny Dean

555-555-5555 (with my real phone number)

jenny@guidetocouponing.com

You, of course, are welcome to put whatever you want on yours – above is just a suggestion on what to write. You might even add something like, "Reward if found."

Chapter 8

Where To Use Coupons

Coupons are accepted at most major national grocery store chains (think Kroger, Albertson's, StopNShop etc), pharmacy store chains (think Walgreens, CVS, Rite Aid, etc.) and the super stores (like Target, Wal-Mart, Kmart, Sears).

Your local stores, restaurants, hardware stores, etc. might also accept coupons. Of course, restaurants are going to accept coupons that they have issued, not manufacturers' coupons. Sometimes large chain restaurants like TGI Friday's will have coupons in the Sunday inserts. They also send coupons to your email address if you are signed up to receive their updates.

To be sure that a store accepts coupons, simply phone them and ask them if they accept manufacturer coupons and while you're at it, you could ask them if they issue store coupons and how you might get your hands on some!

Chapter 9

Rewards Programs

Many chain stores like the pharmacy chain stores and some of the super stores have rewards programs that more often than not involve some sort of card that you scan every time that you check out.

That card is one that you filled out an application for and therefore it's tied to your address, e-mail address and phone number (usually if you have forgotten your card, you can give them your phone number, so they can look it up for you. Having them look it up is important if you get credit for your purchases).

What follows is a list of chain stores that offer reward programs – your local grocery store might have its own reward program. Be sure to ask if you're not sure!

CVS ExtraCare

CVS ExtraCare Card – CVS' ExtraCare program is my favorite reward program out there. In fact, CVS is a store I go to every week because of their awesome deals. Basically, when you shop at CVS with your CVS ExtraCare Card, you can earn 2% back on every purchase and also rewards on prescription purchases – they also have weekly and monthly ExtraBucks Rewards when you purchase select items. Be sure to read the FAQ about CVS ExtraCare to learn all the ins and outs – for example, alcohol and tobacco purchases don't count for the 2% back.

They also will send you special offers and coupons to your inbox, so you can take advantage of extra savings.

However, CVS has made their reward program even better by adding additional incentives to it.

They have a Diabetes Club and a Beauty Club within their ExtraCare program. If you sign up for those (you don't have to be a diabetic to sign up, for example), you will get additional coupons and offers.

- CVS ExtraCare Beauty Club allows you to get $5 ExtraCare Bucks with every $50 spent on beauty products at CVS.

- CVS ExtraCare Diabetes Club - As an ExtraCare Advantage for Diabetes member, you receive extra savings and benefits above and beyond ExtraCare membership.

They also have a Green Bag Tag that works with their ExtraCare program. Every time you make a purchase (limit 1 per day per store) and bring your own green bag, they will scan your Green Bag Tag and every fourth scan you'll get $1 in ExtraCare Bucks.

CVS also has a coupon center (pictured on previous page) that is located at the front of the store – you can scan your CVS ExtraCare card every time you are in the store to get additional store coupons for the week. Be sure to scan it over and over again until the machine tells you that there are no more coupons available that day. There are coupons available every day and usually you can scan it over and over again. Most people just scan it once, not knowing that they will get another round of coupons if they scan it again.

In Chapter 12, I show you how you can take full advantage of a program like CVS ExtraCare.

Erica at iheartcvs.com features the weekly match up deals for CVS ExtraCare and weekly sales.

RiteAid wellness+

When you have a wellness+ account at RiteAid.com you can load coupons to your card that you scan in the store. When you scan your card at checkout, the register will automatically recognize the coupons and subtract them from your total (to make sure you got all your savings just check your receipt because the savings will print on your receipt, so you can verify).

Erica at iheartriteaid.com features the weekly match up deals for RiteAid Wellness+.

Walgreens Register Rewards

Walgreens Register Rewards are coupons that print separately from your register receipt after you purchase qualifying items – they're basically catalinas. The Register Rewards can be used just like cash on your next purchase, although there are some restrictions. You can earn Register Rewards when you make a qualifying purchase of eligible item(s) advertised in Walgreens' Weekly Ad, or an in-store promotion. Limit 1 coupon printed per offer. See coupon for exclusions, limitations and expiration.

iheartwags.com great coupon matchup site for Walgreens Sales and Deals with Register Rewards.

Erica at iheartwags.com will teach you how to coupon effectively at Walgreens stores.

Target Rewards

Target doesn't have a rewards card – but they do offer rewards and deals – their weekly circular will feature them. For example, they often feature things like Buy 2 Get a $5 Target Gift Card – see the photo of the Banana Boat sunscreen promotion below to see what I mean. When you buy 2 Banana Boat sunscreens, you will get a $5 gift card. This is handed to you at checkout after both qualifying sunscreens have been purchased. So think of it like this:

You buy:

Banana Boat Sunscreen $6.49
Banana Boat Sunscreen $6.49

Use two coupons:

-$1 off Banana Boat Sunscreen
-$1 off Banana Boat Sunscreen

Total: $10.98 after coupons – you'll get that $5 gift card, so really you paid $5.98 for two cans of sunscreen or each can for $2.99 – that's a lot better than $6.49!

Kerry at TotallyTarget.com does a great job explaining couponing at Target. You can click here to learn more.

TotallyTarget.com is also a great coupon matchup site for Target. Kerry spends hours scouring the shelves at Target to find the best matchups!

Manufacturers Rewards

Many manufacturers offer reward programs to encourage consumers to not only buy their products but also to acquire consumer's email addresses and sometimes even mailing addresses. Since most manufacturers sell through distribution channels, they rarely have contact with the end user. By establishing a rewards program that encourages the consumer to make contact with them, they are able to have contact with the end user.

Here are some of the rewards programs by manufacturers that I enjoy. There are probably many more – so if you know of some, please email me at info@guidetocouponing.com, so I can list them here.

L'Oreal Gold Rewards - Register to become a Gold Rewards member and receive free hair color products. Buy 5, get one free.

Think Outside the Box!

Considering collecting Coke rewards from parents at your child's school and create an account for the school and redeem the rewards for school stuff for underprivileged kids.... like pens, pencils, books, folders etc....

Pampers Gifts to Grow – Register to enter codes from Pampers products to redeem them for books, toys, sweepstakes entries

My Coke Rewards – Register to enter codes from Coke products to redeem them for free Coke coupons and other great products. If you walk your neighborhood to collect papers for coupon inserts, often time people will have Coke codes (found on Coke products' bottle caps, boxes and the plastic wrap that goes around the 24-packs from Costco).

NatureMade – Register to enter codes from NatureMade vitamin products to redeem them for a $7 coupon and other great products.

Chapter 10

Weekly/BiWeekly/Monthly Sales Flyers

Most weekly flyers usually come out on Sundays. Some companies, like CVS, allow you to see the upcoming weekly flier on Thursday before the new week. There are also certain websites that have them a bit earlier. I like to visit and subscribe to iheartcvs. com for CVS deals – iheartcvs.com always seems to have the CVS weekly flyers 2 weeks in advance. iheartcvs.com also has sister sites for Walgreens and Riteaid, which are iheartwags.com and iheartriteaid.com.

All stores that have websites and also weekly/biweekly/monthly sales flyers will have them online for you to view there – just in case you don't get the newspaper.

Weekly flyers for grocery stores usually come out on Wednesdays – sometimes customer service counters have them the Monday or Sunday before the sale. So you can always ask if the next ad is available to see and usually they will let you have a copy, this way you can plan ahead.

Every store has sales. Many stores, especially grocery stores, have weekly sales flyers to let you know what products are on sale. These weekly flyers are found in newspapers, but are also easily acquired at each individual store. Grocery stores usually have a stack of them near the entrance. CVS, for example, usually has them right above their stack of plastic shopping baskets.

SIDE NOTE! There are also many unadvertised deals in stores – so be sure to check the tags in aisles to take note of any specials you might not have noticed in the weekly circular.

One of my favorite things to do on a Sunday is to get my tea ready and grab my Sharpie marker with all the weekly sale ads. While watching TV and sipping my tea, I love to flip through the weekly sale flyers and circle all the sales that I am interested in.

A great one stop shop for finding weekly flyers is Coupontom.com's Weekly Ad Deals – which includes links to all major grocery store chains, all major pharmacy chains as well as all major super store chains.

Chapter 11

Refunds, Try Me Free, Rebates, Money Back Guarantees

M any times manufacturers will offer incentives for you to try out their products. Those incentives can come in the form of a refund for the total price of the item. For example, you may have seen a Try Me Free sticker or tag hanging on a product or there could be a rebate form, which most often happens with companies such as Proctor and Gamble.

P&G rebates usually involve buying a certain amount to get a certain amount back. For example, if you buy $50 worth of Olay beauty products, then you will get $30 back.

Refunds, Rebates, Try Me Free Forms and Money Back Guarantees usually require sending in the original receipt with the product and purchase priced circled, the product's UPC as a proof of purchase and filling in a form with your contact information. In exchange, depending on the offer at hand, you can receive coupons for free product, free gifts, a check or even a VISA card pre-loaded with your rebate amount on it.

SIDE NOTE! UPC stands for "Universal Product Code". UPCs are found on all grocery store packaging - that's what they scan at checkout to add a product to your transaction. When working with rebates an important database to have at hand is the UPC Database.

Refund Form Locations:

- in the newspaper
- on tear pads
- in magazines
- on specially marked packages
- some stores like Walgreens and RiteAid offer rebate booklets occasionally or monthly, with refunds and items that are free after rebate.
- Try Me Free
    - in the newspaper
    - in the grocery store
    - on tear pads
    - on new products as peelies or hang tags
- RefundCents will have links to forms on the Internet too

Refunds, Try Me Free, Rebates, Money Back Guarantees Tips:

- Keep all receipts because most refunds ask for them
- Mail for your refunds the same day you buy the product
- Collect proofs of purchase - usually the UPC
- Follow the specific directions
- Make copies of your refund submissions before sending them in and date when you sent them in
- Trade refund forms to get a better variety. You can trade through a refund magazine or on-line.

Many people that I know who coupon can make an additional $2,000 a year through rebates - that can be a mortgage payment or a few mortgage payments - so well worth the effort!

Refunds, Rebates, Try Me Free (TMF) Forms and Money Back Guarantees can help you triple your savings.

For example, let's say that Physican's Formula has a TMF sticker on their compact mirror and brush (as pictured below). The compact mirror and brush is on sale for $15.99 and you have a coupon for $3 off any Physican's Formula compact mirror and brush.

You not only got the product on sale and used a coupon, but you are going to get reimbursed for more than the amount you paid for it (usually you are reimbursed for the amount listed on the receipt, or $15.99 in this case, rather than the $12.99 you paid for it)!

Many times you cannot get a rebate without the official form - sometimes it is a little sticker pull from the product and inside the sticker there are directions as to where you can go online to print off the official form. Forms require items like your name, address and zip code and they usually have an optional area where you can include your email address to receive special offers and promotions.

When you have filled out all the information on the refund form, you will send it to the address on the form and they will in turn send your refund offer (whether it be a coupon for free product, a free gift or a check) back to you through the mail.

Refunds usually offer one of four things:

1) CASH - checks or debit cards with a value of $1-$20+
2) Coupons for free products (full size products)
3) Cents or dollars off coupons - usually of high value
4) FREE GIFTS - t-shirts, toys, apparel

IMPORTANT! Be sure to read all the details, effective date periods and follow the directions on the refund, rebate, TMF and money back guarantee forms. Scan copies of the filled out form, the original receipt(s) and the UPCs before you send it all in. Make a note of when you sent it in and keep track of it until you receive it back in the mail. If you followed all the directions, you should get your rebate back in the mail.

Chapter 12

How To Stack Coupons
And Maximize Your Savings

Stacking coupons is one the best ways to get items for free or for next to nothing. What does it mean to stack coupons? If you've watched the Extreme Couponing show, then you might have noticed that the couponer literally hands the cashier a stack of coupons when s/he is ready to check out. That's one of the reasons it is called stacking coupons, but another is because you can sometimes use two coupons on one purchase. In other words, **you can stack a manufacturer's coupon with a store coupon** when you purchase something.

In order to easily locate coupons to stack with sales prices, you'll want to reference a coupon database so that you don't spend hours searching through your coupons. God bless the invention of the Internet for making this a lot easier on us.

Coupon Database

The coupon database that I like to use the most is CouponTom.com. Simply type the brand or the product that you're looking for a coupon for in the search box and it will auto populate results as you type – BRILLIANT!

After emailing with Tom, I discovered that he started the site because he wanted an easy way to find coupons. He is a computer programmer, so he took on the challenge and boy - am I glad he did! Thanks, Tom!

CouponTom.com will even tell you where expired coupons are – you have to sign up for an account through the website for this feature though. An account is free though! You might be interested in expired coupons because a lot of stores will accept coupons 1-5 days after they expire depending on where they fall in the month. In order to make sure your store accepts expired coupons, be sure to ask the manager what their policy is. Some stores' policies are to accept coupons two weeks after the coupon expires.

Coupontom.com allows you to browse all current coupons; browse coupons that are expiring soon, quickly search for BOGO and free coupons and more. Have some fun exploring the site...and while you're there, you might thank Tom for creating it!

One of the best ways to maximize your savings is to double, triple or quadruple your savings by taking advantage of several kinds of savings like coupons, sales, rebates and try me free forms. It's important to know the store's policy when it comes to matching competitors' prices, doubling coupons, etc. so you can always land the best savings.

Savings x 2 = Product on Sale + Manufacturer's Coupon

When you coordinate a product on sale with a coupon, you end up doubling your savings.

So, let's say that Larabars are on sales from $1.49 to $1 each.

You buy 4 Larabars @ $1/each = $4
– $1 WYB (when you buy) 4 Larabars
Final Price = $3 or 75¢ per Larabar

Whereas if you used that coupon when the Larabars were regularly priced, you would pay:

You buy 4 Larabars @ $1.49/each = $5.96
– $1 WYB 4 Larabars
Final Price = $4.96 or $1.24 per Larabar

I like savings x 2 better – don't you?!

Here's another example:

Tylenol Precise
Retail Price: $7.49
Sale Price: $5.99
Coupon: $5.00
Total: $0.99

Savings x 2 = Double Coupons

Another way to double your savings is by shopping at stores that double coupons.

Some grocery store chains and some super stores (Kmart comes to mind) offer double coupons. One of my grocery store chains in town doubles any coupon 50 cents or less. So, for example, if Colgate is on sale for $2.99 and I have a 50 cent coupon then it double to $1 at the register and my final price would be $1.99. Sometimes you might have a 45 cent off coupon and a 75 cent off coupon. If you are in a store that doubles, then using the 45 cent off coupon would be wiser, because it will give you 90 cents off the sales price, whereas the 75 cent one will only give you 75 cents off.

Some stores like Kmart offer Double Coupons up to a certain dollar amount – in other words, they might double up to $2. They do not do this all the time, but will advertise in your local paper or your local ad (which you can access online) that it is happening that week.

I love double coupons. I cannot tell you how many bags of frozen veggies I have gotten for free or nearly free because of coupon doubling. For example, if bags of Bird's Eye veggies are on sale for 79 cents and I have a coupon for 35 cents off of one. When that coupon doubles, it doubles to 70 cents – so the final price for that bag of peas is only nine cents! If you are a mom and making your own baby food, this can be killer!

One of the ways to make the most out of your coupons regardless if they double or not is to buy the smallest size of the product. However, many manufacturers do put size limitations on the coupon itself – so be sure to read the coupon to see if there is a size limit. Let's look at a scenario for Palmolive dishwashing soap. Let's say that the store sells three sizes and all three sizes are on sale for these prices:

Palmolive 20 oz. – 99 cents
Palmolive 40 oz. - $1.99
Palmolive 60 oz. - $3.99

If I have a 50 cent coupon for any Palmolive and the store doubles, then I will get the 20 oz for free, whereas I would get the 60 oz for $2.99. I would rather buy 3 of the smaller sizes and get them all for free rather than one of the big sizes.

If you've watched Extreme Couponing on TLC, then you have seen how people come home with thousands of dollars worth of groceries for just pennies on the dollar. It might seem impossible, but it is very possible.

Here's a scenario if you're shopping at Kmart, for example:

Kmart Free Grocery Scenario:

Sale Price = $1.00
Manufacturer's Coupon = $0.50
Store Doubles Coupons 50 cents or less = -$0.50
Final Price = $0.00 plus tax

Savings x 3 = Product on Sale + Manufacturer's Coupon + Store Coupon

When you coordinate a product on sale with a manufacturer's coupon and a store coupon, you triple your savings.

Let's look at this hypothetical deal at Target for this. Remember that Target coupon from Chapter 1 (it's pictured again here).

Let's say that you have $1 coupons for Tidy Cats litter.

Tidy Cats litter is also on sale for $11.49, marked down from $12.99.

So, to use the $5 off, you buy 2 Tidy Cats litter bags or buckets.

Tidy Cats litter 35lb bag $11.49 x 2 = $22.98
— $1 Tidy Cats litter manufacturer's coupon
— $1 Tidy Cats litter manufacturer's coupon
— $5 Target Coupon WYB 2 Tidy Cats litter
Pay $15.98 plus tax instead of $22.98 plus tax

Savings x 4 = Product on Sale + Manufacturer's Coupon + Store Coupon + Rebate/TMF

When you coordinate a product on sale with a manufacturer's coupon and a store coupon and then send in a rebate or TMF form for that item, you quadruple your savings.

Let's look at the following scenario. Let's say Physician's Formula Youthful Wear Concealer is on sale for $15.99:

Physician's Formula Youthful Wear Concealer = $15.99
— $3 off any Physician's Formula Youthful Wear Concealer (manufacturer's coupon)
— $5 off any $10 or more purchase of Physician's Formula (store coupon)
You Pay OOP (out-of-pocket): $7.99

Then you send in for the TMF (Try Me Free) Rebate on Physician's Formula Youthful Wear Concealer (notice the TMF sticker on the package) and get a $15.99 check back 6-8 weeks later.

You only paid $7.99 after coupons, but were reimbursed $15.99 – so technically you made $8.

Here's another situation where you can earn savings times four – but this is through a store rewards program.

Let's look at this hypothetical deal at RiteAid with their Ups (Ups are part of RiteAid's Reward program) – this was actually a deal once upon a time. You netted a pound of pistachios for .99 (Reg $8.99).

Wonderful Pistachios 1 lb bag $4.99
— $1 printable
Pay $3.99
Get a $3 Ups
Final price .99

Here's another example using CVS ExtraCare Bucks:

Revlon Nail Enamel is on sale for $4.99 and WYB 1 Revlon Nail Enamel you get $3 ECB back. The limit on the number you can purchase is 6. You scan your card at the CVS coupon center and get a CVS coupon for $3 off any $10 cosmetic purchase. So, you buy:

3 Revlon Nail Enamels @ $4.99 each
— $1 off any Revlon Nail purchase (manufacturer's coupons)
— $1 off any Revlon Nail purchase (manufacturer's coupons)
— $1 off any Revlon Nail purchase (manufacturer's coupons)
— $3 off any $10 cosmetic purchase (CVS coupon)
Pay $8.97 and get back $9 in ECBs

That same week, CVS might have a deal on Almay — WYB $10 worth of Almay cosmetics, you get $4 in ECB. So, you buy:

2 Almay yeshadows @ $5.69 each
— $1 off any Almay cosmetic (manufacturer's coupon printed online)
— $1 off any Almay cosmetic (manufacturer's coupon printed online)
— $3 off any $10 cosmetic purchase (CVS coupon)
Pay $6.38 and get back $4 in ECBs to use on your next purchase

Savings x 5 = Product on Sale + Manufacturer's Coupon + Store Coupon + Rewards + Rebate/TMF

When you take advantage of the stores' rewards programs or even manufacturers' rewards programs in accordance with your deals, you get savings times five!

Let's look again at the scenario above with Physician's Formula Youthful Wear Concealer. Let's say that CVS is offering $7 ExtraCare Bucks when you purchase $15 worth of Physician's Formula.

Physician's Formula Youthful Wear Concealer = $15.99
— $3 off any Physician's Formula Youthful Wear Concealer (manufacturer's coupon)
— $5 off any $10 or more purchase of Physician's Formula (store coupon)
You Pay OOP: $7.99

You receive $7 in ExtraCare Bucks (printed at the bottom of your receipt) for buying $15 worth of Physican's Formula. So really...

Your Final Cost before TMF = 99 cents

Then you send in for the TMF Rebate on Physician's Formula Youthful Wear Concealer (notice the TMF sticker on the package) and get a $15.99 check back 6-8 weeks later.

Remember that your final cost was $0.99 after coupons and rewards, but you were reimbursed $15.99 — so technically you made $15 from this purchase.

This is how you make money couponing!

Clearance Items

Clearance items are usually located on the back end caps in stores like Wal-Mart, Target, CVS, etc. They might also be located in the store itself – as indicated in the picture. If you cannot locate the clearance items, just ask an employee to point out where to find them in the store.

What's the best part? Coupons can be used on clearance items! So taking the L-Lysine photo example from CVS as pictured.

If I have a $1 off any Nature Made Vitamin, then the L-Lysine ends up being $1.37 – that's a lot better than paying $9.49 for it! Often items are on clearance because they do not sell well at that location or CVS, for example, is getting them out of inventory.

An even better scenario is if Nature Made vitamins are on sale that week as B1G1.

Here's how that would work:

Nature Made L-Lysine @ $2.37 x 2 = $4.74
– $2.37 for B1G1
– $1 on any Nature Made Product
– $1 on any Nature Made Product (yes, CVS lets you use 1 coupon per item even on B1G1 sales)
Pay $0.37 for 2 bottles!

...and don't forget that those bottles of Nature Made will have codes on them that you can enter on Nature Made's website for rewards!

You can look for these deals in the store, but there are also awesome coupon match-up sites that lay out these scenarios for you. I have included a list of them in the resource section.

My sister-in-law takes L-Lysine, so when I brought home 8 bottles of Lysine for next to nothing for her – she was pretty excited.

Rainchecks

Most stores offer rainchecks. When a product is out of stock and it's on sale or there is a special offer on that particular product, a store like CVS will issue a raincheck which comes in the form of a slip of paper. All you usually have to do is ask the employee for a raincheck for the out-of-stock item.

Sometimes they might have it in the back of the store, and if so they will go and get it for you. But if they are completely sold out then a store employee manually writes in the details of the sale on their pre-made store raincheck pad of paper – they then give you that slip. You must then present that slip the next time you are in the store to obtain the deal of the raincheck.

Rainchecks can be good for 30 days or not have an expiration date – so these can be like gold because you can wait until there is a killer high-value coupon that comes out and then use your raincheck with it to maximize your savings.

Sales Tax

Whether or not you are charged sales tax on the subtotal depends on your state. For example, I live in Kansas City – which is located in Kansas and Missouri. If my subtotal is $0.00 in Missouri, then my total is $0.00. However, if my subtotal is $0.00 in Kansas, I am still charged tax on taxable items. Therefore, whenever I can, I shop in Missouri. I have paid as much as $3 on a zero subtotal in Kansas – YUCK!

Multiple Transactions

To maximize savings, I often do multiple transactions. For example, if I have two $5 off a $20 purchase coupons (these coupons sometimes appear in our local newspaper for CVS) then I will do 2 transactions, each totaling just over $20.

Another reason to do multiple transactions is because some store coupon policies might say that they can double only 20 coupons per transaction and you can only use 1 like coupon per transaction. In other words, sometimes P&G coupons limit you the number of coupons in a transaction. Let's say you're buy 5 tubes of Crest toothpaste and the coupons say, "Limit 4 Like Coupons in same shopping trip." You can still buy the 5 tubes of Crest, but you can only use 4 of your 5 coupons because of the limitations on the coupon.

Chapter 13

Your First Trip To The Store

Before I go to the store, I always prepare so that I spend less time in the store. I not only organize my coupons, but also lay them out in an Excel spreadsheet. You can download this spreadsheet here from my website – and then just plug in the numbers to get an idea of how much you are going to owe after coupons.

The best way to get your first real deal is to buy a product that is on sale and that you have a coupon for. For example, if Crest toothpaste is on sale for $2.99 and you have a $1 off one tube of Crest, then you're paying $1.99 for that tube, rather than the $5.99 full retail price. Of course, if you have 10 coupons for Crest and love Crest then go ahead and buy 10 tubes of Crest – after all, you are getting them all for just $1.99 each. Be sure to read the fine print on the coupons though – as sometimes it limits you to four per transaction or there could be other limitations.

I like to go to the store, when possible, during down times – 10am in the morning, 7pm at night. I try to avoid heavy traffic hours – Saturday nights are also good as well as early Sunday mornings when people are at church! The less people waiting in line behind you, the better. Fellow shoppers waiting to check out can get easily annoyed by couponers – especially if they are not organized. Just think about it - no one likes to wait around while someone fishes through a coupon binder to find the right coupons. So be sure to approach the register completely organized and ready to go.

But this is the first essential step to couponing – matching coupons with sale products. If you do this and nothing else, you will probably end up saving 50% or more on most of your purchases.

One of the best rules of thumb is to always have your coupon binder or accordion file with you - I always bring mine wherever I go as there have been too many times that I was bummed that I didn't have my coupons with me and ended up paying full price (which drives me crazy especially when I KNOW I have a coupon for it).

How to Organize Trip to the Store

I like to visit coupon matchup sites for specific stores like CVS and Target (you can see a list of coupon match up sites like RefundCents and iheartcvs.com in the resource section at the end of this book).

I also like to go through weekly flyers that I find in the newspaper and circle the deals I am interested in – sometimes I can skip this step because RefundCents and iheartcvs.com already have it all laid out for me.

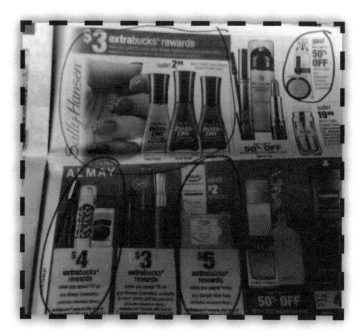

Once I have gone through the flyers and the matchup sites, I then hop on my computer and visit a site like CouponTom.com to see if there are any additional coupons available for the items on sale that I was interested in. While the coupon matchup sites usually do this for you – sometimes they miss a few coupons that you might have, so I do this extra step to make sure I am taking full advantage of savings.

As I work my way through the matchup websites, coupon database and weekly flyers, I like to organize my transactions with the Guide to Couponing Excel Spreadsheet. For example, here's a screen print of a recent trip I planned for CVS:

	price	coupons	cvs cpn	ecb	ecb needed
Coppertone	$ 8.99	$ 1.00	$4.00	$3.00	$3.99
Salonpas	$ 1.87			$ 1.87	$ 1.87
Almay	$ 10.00		$ 3.00	$ 4.00	$ 7.00
	$ 20.86			$ 8.87	$ 12.86

You'll see that I planned on buying Coppertone, Salonpas and Almay.

Coupons - I had a $1 manufacturer's coupon for Coppertone. I also had 2 store coupons – one for a $4 off $20 purchase and another for $3 off a $10 cosmetic purchase.

ECBs – That week, CVS was offering ECBs on Coppertone ($3 ECBs WYB 1 @ $8.99), Salonpas ($1.87 ECB WYB 1 @ $1.87) and Almay ($4 ECBs WYB $10 worth of Almay).

So instead of spending $20.86, I spent $12.86 in ECBs that I had from a previous shopping trip and then got back $8.87 in ECBs to use on my next trip.

Once everything is organized - you have planned your trip and all your coupons are organized for the products you plan on buying, head to the store - and if you can make the trip worthwhile gas wise, all the better. In other words, I try to go to CVS, for example, once a week - or twice a week if I am driving by one on my way to another appointment.

Your First Trip Checklist:

- Bring Your Coupon Binder or Accordion File
- Bring a Printed Out Version of Your Planned Trip to the Store or load it on your phone and have it ready to got
- Have the coupons for each transaction paper-clipped together
- Print out the Coupon Policy of the store you're visiting and have it with you should any problems arise

I like to have my trip planned out with each transaction paper clipped and ready to go. Having all your coupons pulled for the products you are purchasing is the right and courteous thing to do BEFORE you get in line for checkout. It's courteous to the cashier and the people waiting behind you in line.

SIDE NOTE! I remember one time when I was behind a fellow couponer and she was not only disorganized, but she stood there and did multiple transactions before the people buying a pack of gum could complete their transaction and get out of there. If there are people behind me in line and I plan on doing multiple transactions (as I often do – so I can maximize coupons like $4 off a $20 purchase), I always step back into line for the next transaction. There are many people out there that find couponers annoying and if we are courteous of others, it will help people respect couponers more. Of course, a savvy cashier will also take control of a situation like that and ask for additional cashiers to help people get rung up or will ask the couponers to step back in line.

Steps to Effective Couponing:

1. Match manufacturers coupons with products on sale

2. Match store coupons with products on sale

3. Match store rewards and/or manufacturer's rewards with products on sale that you also have coupons for

4. Find rebates for products on sale that you have coupons for as well

If it is a product that you use on a regular basis, stock up on it! You want to buy as many as you and/or your family needs until there is another sale. Again, avoiding buying items at full price is the goal with couponing. As a rule of thumb, most items go on sale every 6-8 weeks.

By buying multiple tubes of toothpaste for example, you are stocking up on toothpaste and will therefore be starting your "stock pile" that you have probably heard of on TLC's popular TV Show, Extreme Couponing.

Great Couponer Matchup Sites, Printable Coupons, Coupon Databases Websites

There are two websites that I visit every day to figure out what the best deals are – these might not be your ideal sites – so I have included a list of sites below so that you can explore them and figure out which ones work for you.

However, the ones that I frequent are RefundCents. com and also iheartcvs.com. The ladies who run these sites do an excellent job at keeping up with matching weekly sales flyers with coupons – so that I don't have to!

General Coupon Matchup Websites:

- RefundCents
- TotallyTarget
- Weusecoupons.com
- iheartcvs.com
- Hot Coupon World
- Fat Wallet
- AfullCup.com
- CouponSuzy.com

GuidetoCouponing.com Reader Lisa says, "I subscribe to what I consider to be the best email newsletter around www.MomsNeedToKnow.com ....sends out a daily newsletter that is easy to read and click thru and lists daily deals. I have saved so much $$$ using her newsletter when I was shopping for birthday gifts for my kids. She alerted to sales I had no idea about and was able to save about $100 per child by using her info."

- Hip2Save.com
- MomsNeedToKnow.com
- Couponmom.com

Coupon Matchup Websites for CVS:

- RefundCents
- iheartcvs.com
- Fat Wallet
- AfullCup.com
- Couponmom.com

Coupon Matchup Websites for RiteAid:

- RefundCents
- iheartriteaid.com
- Fat Wallet
- AfullCup.com
- Couponmom.com

Coupon Matchup Websites for Target:

- TotallyTarget
- RefundCents
- Fat Wallet
- AfullCup.com
- Couponmom.com

Coupon Matchup Websites for Walgreens:

- RefundCents
- iheartwags.com
- Fat Wallet
- AfullCup.com
- Couponmom.com

Popular Coupon Clipping Services:

- CouponDede.com
- The Coupon Master
- The Coupon Clippers

GuidetoCouponing.com Reader Micki says, "I like to subscribe to Couponmom.com. You sign up for free and under your account there is an option to enter your store' loyalty account numbers (usually on the back of the card). Then you just "grab" the coupon from the couponmom website and it automatically (somehow) adds it to your customer card. Then when you are at checkout and they scan your store loyalty card, it automatically deducts the savings (if you bought the items the coupons were for, of course).

Printable Coupons:

- Coupons.com
- Red Plum
- SmartSource
- Individual Manufacturer's websites
- Store Websites
- Home Made Simple
- Coolsavings.com
- Albertsons.com
- Couponsurfer.com
- Kroger.com
- BoxTops4Education.com
- BettyCrocker.com
- Eclip.com
- Pillsbury.com
- EatBetterAmerica.com
- ValPak.com
- Target.com
- CVS.com
- Couponnetwork.com
- Couponmom.com

Grocery Deals by State

- Couponmom.com

eCoupons

- SavingStar

Coupon Databases:

- CouponTom

Local Coupons for Restaurants and More

- Google Offers
- Groupon
- Living Social
- Morgan's Deals (only in Austin, Colorado Springs, Fort Collins, Kansas City, St. Louis)

- Mamasource by Mamapedia
- DealSaver.com

Great Online Couponing Websites:

- RetailMeNot.com - EXCELLENT site for discounts online as well as coupon codes, etc.

Online Pet Food Websites:

- Mrchewy.com – free shipping at $49. $4.95 flat rate for orders under $49. Get 10% off your first order from @mrchewy by using promo code: JENN7837 or 15% off first autoship order (you can cancel at any time) – you could always do your first order at 10% off and then use the 15% on the second one. Or combine the 10% and 15% off in your first order. Unsure about sales tax – I would think only FL?
- Wag.com – free shipping at $49. Sales tax in WA, KS, NY, NJ, and PA. (They are affiliated with amazon.com) 15% discount with code 15WAG. A site like RetailMeNot.com can help you find another coupon code if WAGFOOD12 is expired by the time you read this book.
- Waggintails.com – free shipping at $59.99. Sign up for email and get a discount code. Like their Facebook page and they post other discount codes. Unsure about sales tax – company is in MA.
- Doggiefood.com – free shipping at $49.99. 10% off for new customers with code NEW10. Like their Facebook page for future promo codes. They also have bird, bunny and some horse supplies. They are located in RI.
- Petflow.com – free shipping at $59. Or free shipping at $49 with promo code FBFANS. Or free shipping on any three items with code FREE3. Like their Facebook page for promo codes. Sales tax in NY, NJ and NV.

Coupon Policies

- CVS Coupon Policy
- Target's Coupon Policy
- Wal-mart Coupon Policy
- Rite-Aid Coupon Policy
- Walgreens Coupon Policy

800 Numbers

http://householdproducts.nlm.nih.gov/cgi-bin/household/list?tbl=TblBrands&alpha=A

Company Addresses:

http://householdproducts.nlm.nih.gov/cgi-bin/household/list?tbl=TblBrands&alpha=A

UPC Database:

http://www.upcdatabase.com/

Thank You for Reading Couponing for the Beginner: A Guide to Couponing for the Uninitiated

A sincere thank you to you for reading Couponing for the Beginner: A Guide to Couponing for the Uninitiated.

I hope that you will share your first couponing experience with us on GuideToCouponing.com in days, months and years to come. You are always welcome to submit a story about your coupon journey to me through e-mail at info@guidetocouponing.com – if you want to share it on the site.

I would like to take this opportunity to say again that I spent a lot of time and effort creating this book and would appreciate it if you would respect my work by not sharing or distributing the book to anyone else without my permission.

If you have any suggestions, tips or criticisms of this book, please do not hesitate to contact me at info@guidetocouponing.com with any comments!

I am also always on the lookout for testimonials for the guide, if you are up for sending a testimonial, please think about the following questions:

- What kind of doubts did you have before starting to read this guide? Be honest.
- How did the guide deliver on its promises?
- Who would you recommend this to and why?

While I do my very best to provide all the information that you need to get started couponing for a profit, I am only human and might have forgotten something.

Do you have any questions that I haven't addressed in this *Couponing for the Beginner: A Guide to Couponing for the Uninitiated*? Please don't hesitate to ask me any questions by sending me an email to info@guidetocouponing.com I can make this book better if I understand what I might need to add.

Note for Hard Copy Readers: If you contact me at info@guidetocouponing.com I will send you a digital version of the book (in PDF form) that has all the clickable links - so that you don't have to spend your time searching and typing in links, rather you can just click through!

Thank you again for your purchase and I look forward to hearing about your great deals and steals!

6781

Made in the USA
Lexington, KY
18 February 2015